RESPIRATORY CARE IN HOME AND COMMUNITY SETTINGS

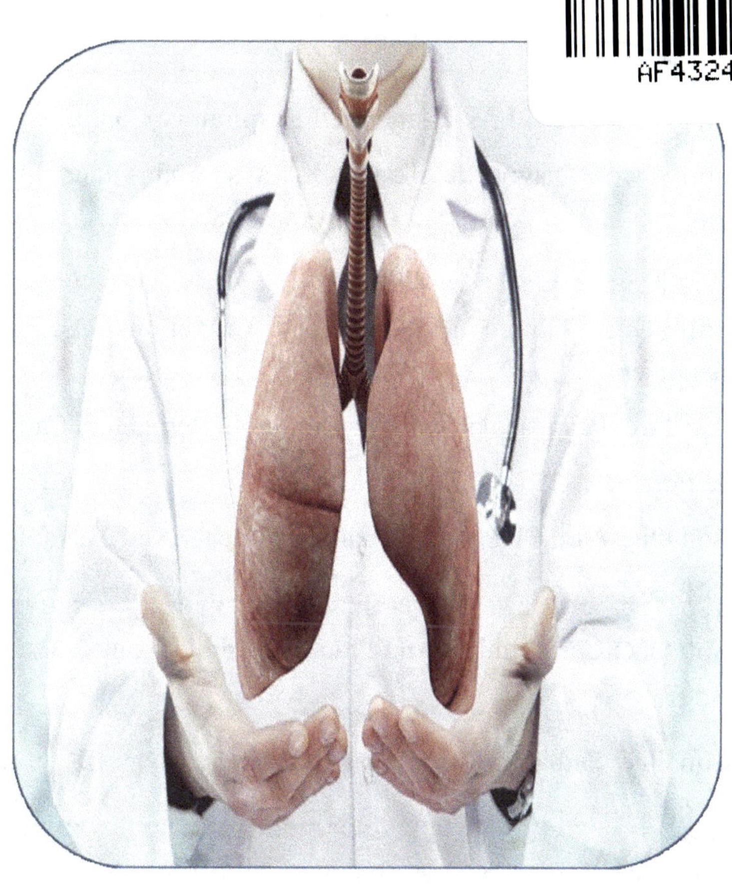

TABLE OF CONTENTS

<u>**COURSE OVERVIEW**</u>

This comprehensive course is designed to provide healthcare professionals with in-depth knowledge and practical skills for managing respiratory conditions in home and community settings. Through a combination of theoretical learning and practical case studies, participants will be equipped to deliver high-quality, patient-centered respiratory care outside of hospital environments.

<u>**COURSE OBJECTIVE**</u>

By the end of this course, participants will be able to Understand Respiratory Anatomy and Physiology, Perform Comprehensive Clinical Assessments, Interpret Diagnostic Imaging, Manage Common Respiratory Conditions, Provide Pediatric Respiratory Care, Incorporate Innovations in Respiratory Care, Promote Patient-Centered Care, and Apply Knowledge through Case Studies. This course is ideal for respiratory therapists, doctors, nurses, and other healthcare providers who wish to enhance their expertise in respiratory care and improve patient outcomes in home and community settings. Through interactive sessions, hands-on practice, and evidence-based learning, participants will gain the confidence and competence to excel in this vital area of healthcare.

<u>**COURSE MATERIALS**</u>

To learn this course, **healthcare providers/ participants** must be provided with materials like a Pen, pencil, notebook, and notepad to better understand and make it easy for them to learn.

INTRODUCTION

Respiratory care is a crucial aspect of healthcare, especially for patients receiving treatment in home and community settings. The shift towards more patient-centered care models has increased the demand for healthcare providers who are knowledgeable and skilled in managing respiratory conditions outside traditional hospital environments. This book aims to serve as an all-encompassing guide for respiratory therapists, doctors, nurses, and other healthcare providers, offering in-depth knowledge and practical advice on respiratory care in these settings.

Respiratory conditions can significantly impact the quality of life for patients and pose unique challenges for healthcare providers. The complexity of these conditions necessitates a thorough understanding of respiratory anatomy and physiology, clinical assessment techniques, diagnostic tools, and effective treatment modalities. This book is designed to bridge the knowledge gap, providing healthcare providers with the information and tools they need to deliver high-quality respiratory care.

The goal of this book is not only to impart knowledge but also to inspire and empower healthcare providers to deliver compassionate and effective respiratory care in home and community settings. By the end of this guide, readers will have a comprehensive understanding of respiratory care, from the basics of respiratory anatomy and physiology to the complexities of diagnosing and treating respiratory conditions.

MODULE ONE

LESSON ONE: RESPIRATORY CARE IN HOME AND COMMUNITY SETTINGS

The practice of respiratory care has evolved significantly over the years, moving beyond the confines of hospitals and clinics to encompass home and community settings. This shift is driven by several factors, including advancements in medical technology, a growing emphasis on patient-centered care, and the increasing prevalence of chronic respiratory conditions. This lesson provides an overview of respiratory care in these non-traditional settings, highlighting the unique challenges and opportunities they present.

The Evolution of Respiratory Care

Historically, respiratory care was predominantly provided in hospitals and specialized clinics. However, with the advent of portable medical devices, telemedicine, and other technological innovations, it is now feasible to deliver high-quality respiratory care in patients' homes and community-based facilities. This evolution has been further accelerated by the rising number of patients with chronic respiratory diseases, such as chronic obstructive pulmonary disease (COPD) and asthma, who require ongoing management and support.

Importance of Respiratory Care in Home and Community Settings

Providing respiratory care in home and community settings offers numerous benefits, including improved patient comfort and convenience, reduced healthcare costs, and better patient outcomes. Patients often feel more at ease in their own homes, which can enhance their overall well-being and adherence to treatment plans. Additionally, home-based care can help reduce the burden on healthcare facilities, freeing up resources for acute and critical care needs.

Key Components of Respiratory Care

Effective respiratory care in home and community settings involves several key components:

- Patient Assessment: A thorough assessment of the patient's respiratory status, including history taking, physical examination, and the use of diagnostic tools.
- Treatment Planning: Developing individualized treatment plans based on the patient's specific needs and preferences.
- Education and Training: Educating patients and their caregivers about respiratory conditions, treatment options, and self-management techniques.
- Monitoring and Follow-Up: Regular monitoring of the patient's condition and adjustment of treatment plans as necessary.

Roles and Responsibilities of Healthcare Providers

Healthcare providers play a crucial role in delivering respiratory care in home and community settings. Their responsibilities include:

- Conducting Assessments: Performing comprehensive assessments to determine the patient's respiratory status and identify any issues.

- Developing Treatment Plans: Creating tailored treatment plans that address the patient's unique needs.
- Providing Education: Educating patients and their caregivers on how to manage respiratory conditions effectively.
- Monitoring Progress: Continuously monitoring the patient's progress and making necessary adjustments to the treatment plan.
- Coordinating Care: Collaborating with other healthcare professionals to ensure a holistic approach to patient care.

Challenges and Opportunities

While respiratory care in home and community settings offers many benefits, it also presents certain challenges. These may include:

- Resource Limitations: Limited access to medical equipment and supplies in home settings.
- Caregiver Burden: The need for caregivers to be adequately trained and supported.
- Communication Barriers: Ensuring effective communication between patients, caregivers, and healthcare providers.

Despite these challenges, the opportunities for improving patient care and outcomes are substantial. By leveraging technology, enhancing patient education, and fostering strong collaboration among healthcare providers, we can overcome these challenges and deliver high-quality respiratory care in home and community settings.

Respiratory care in home and community settings is an essential component of modern healthcare. It offers numerous benefits to patients and healthcare systems alike, but it requires a comprehensive and coordinated approach to be effective. The subsequent lessons of this book will delve deeper into the various aspects of respiratory care, providing healthcare providers with the knowledge and tools they need to excel in this field.

DISCUSSION QUESTIONS

- How can healthcare providers effectively educate patients and their families about managing respiratory conditions in home and community settings?
- What are the primary challenges in delivering respiratory care outside of hospital settings, and how can they be overcome?

LESSON TWO: UNDERSTANDING THE RESPIRATORY SYSTEM; ANATOMY AND PHYSIOLOGY

A thorough understanding of the respiratory system's anatomy and physiology is foundational for any healthcare provider involved in respiratory care. This lesson provides a detailed overview of the respiratory system, including its structure, function, and the physiological processes involved in respiration.

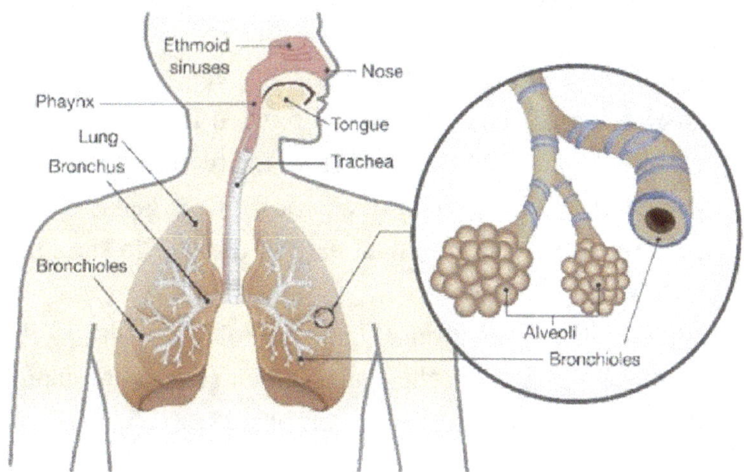

Structure of the Respiratory System

The respiratory system is comprised of several key structures, each playing a vital role in the process of respiration. These structures include:

- Nose and Nasal Cavity: The primary entry point for air, where it is filtered, warmed, and humidified.
- Pharynx and Larynx: Pathways for air to travel from the nasal cavity to the trachea; the larynx also houses the vocal cords.
- Trachea: A tube that directs air from the larynx to the bronchi.

- Bronchi and Bronchioles: Branching airways that lead air into the lungs.
- Lungs: The main organs of respiration, consisting of alveoli where gas exchange occurs.
- Diaphragm and Intercostal Muscles: Muscles that facilitate breathing by changing the volume of the thoracic cavity.

Function of the Respiratory System

The primary function of the respiratory system is to facilitate the exchange of gases, oxygen and carbon dioxide between the external environment and the bloodstream. This process involves several key steps:

- Ventilation: The movement of air into and out of the lungs.
- Gas Exchange: The diffusion of oxygen from the alveoli into the blood and carbon dioxide from the blood into the alveoli.
- Transport of Gases: The circulation of oxygenated blood to the tissues and the return of carbon dioxide to the lungs for exhalation.
- Regulation of Breathing: The control of breathing by the respiratory centers in the brain, which respond to changes in blood gas levels.

Physiological Processes

Understanding the physiological processes involved in respiration is essential for recognizing and managing respiratory conditions. Key processes include:

- Oxygenation: The uptake of oxygen by the blood in the lungs and its delivery to tissues.
- Ventilation-Perfusion Matching: The efficient matching of air flow (ventilation) and blood flow (perfusion) in the lungs to optimize gas exchange.

- Acid-Base Balance: The role of the respiratory system in maintaining the body's acid-base balance by regulating carbon dioxide levels.

Clinical Implications

Knowledge of respiratory anatomy and physiology is critical for healthcare providers as it informs the assessment, diagnosis, and treatment of respiratory conditions. For example:

- Recognizing Abnormalities: Identifying deviations from normal respiratory function, such as hypoxemia or hypercapnia.
- Guiding Treatment: Understanding how different treatments, such as supplemental oxygen or bronchodilators, affect respiratory physiology.
- Patient Education: Explaining respiratory conditions and treatments to patients in a way that is understandable and relevant to their experience.

A solid grasp of the respiratory system's anatomy and physiology provides the foundation for effective respiratory care. The next lesson will build on this knowledge, exploring clinical assessment techniques, diagnostic tools, and treatment strategies in greater detail.

DISCUSSION QUESTIONS

- How does the anatomy of the respiratory system influence the pathophysiology of common respiratory conditions?
- What role does understanding respiratory physiology play in the effective treatment and management of respiratory diseases?

MODULE TWO

LESSON ONE: CLINICAL ASSESSMENT OF RESPIRATORY CONDITIONS

Accurate and comprehensive clinical assessment is the cornerstone of effective respiratory care. This lesson focuses on the techniques and tools used to assess respiratory conditions, including history taking, physical examination, and the interpretation of clinical signs and symptoms.

Past medical history	Any previous operations or procedures
	Any use of oxygen or continuous/bi-level positive airway pressure devices (BiPAP or CPAP)
	Any chronic disorders such as asthma, COPD, cystic fibrosis
Drug history	Prescribed drugs, over the counter drugs, recreational drugs, herbal remedies, include allergies
Family history	Tuberculosis, cystic fibrosis, emphysema, allergies, asthma, bronchiectasis, clotting disorders (risk of pulmonary embolism)
Social history	Smoking, alcohol, consider diet and lifestyle, occupational history, travel history, sexual history
Systematic enquiry	Run through common symptoms of all the systems

History Taking

A thorough patient history is the first step in assessing respiratory conditions. Key components of the history include:

- Chief Complaint: Understanding the primary reason for the patient's visit, such as shortness of breath, cough, or chest pain.
- History of Present Illness: Detailed information about the onset, duration, and characteristics of the symptoms.
- Past Medical History: Relevant medical history, including previous respiratory conditions, surgeries, and hospitalizations.
- Family History: Any family history of respiratory diseases or conditions.

- Social History: Factors such as smoking, occupational exposures, and living conditions that may impact respiratory health.
- Review of Systems: A systematic review of other body systems to identify any related or contributing factors.

Physical Examination

The physical examination is crucial for identifying clinical signs of respiratory conditions. Key components include:

- Inspection: Observing the patient's overall appearance, respiratory effort, and any visible signs of distress.
- Palpation: Assessing for tenderness, masses, or abnormal movements in the chest.
- Percussion: Tapping on the chest to evaluate underlying structures and detect abnormalities.
- Auscultation: Listening to the breath sounds using a stethoscope to identify normal and abnormal sounds, such as wheezing, crackles, or diminished breath sounds.

Clinical Signs and Symptoms

Recognizing the clinical signs and symptoms of respiratory conditions is essential for accurate diagnosis. Common signs and symptoms include:

- Dyspnea: Shortness of breath or difficulty breathing.
- Cough: A persistent or productive cough.
- Chest Pain: Pain that may be associated with breathing or coughing.
- Cyanosis: A bluish discoloration of the skin and mucous membranes due to low oxygen levels.
- Clubbing: Enlargement of the fingertips, often associated with chronic hypoxia.

Diagnostic Tools

In addition to history taking and physical examination, various diagnostic tools are used to assess respiratory conditions. These include:

- Pulse Oximetry: A non-invasive method to measure oxygen saturation levels in the blood.
- Spirometry: A test that measures lung function, including the volume and flow of air during inhalation and exhalation.
- Arterial Blood Gases (ABGs): A blood test that provides information about oxygenation, ventilation, and acid-base status.
- Chest X-Ray: Imaging to visualize the structures of the chest and identify abnormalities such as pneumonia, pleural effusion, or lung masses.

Case Example

Consider a patient presenting with shortness of breath and a productive cough. The clinical assessment would involve:

- Taking a detailed history to understand the onset and progression of symptoms, any previous respiratory conditions, and potential exposure to respiratory irritants.
- Performing a physical examination to identify signs such as increased respiratory effort, use of accessory muscles, and abnormal breath sounds.
- Using diagnostic tools like pulse oximetry to assess oxygen saturation, spirometry to evaluate lung function, and a chest X-ray to visualize any structural abnormalities.

Clinical assessment is a vital component of respiratory care. By gathering comprehensive information through history taking, physical examination, and the use of diagnostic tools, healthcare providers can accurately diagnose and manage respiratory conditions.

DISCUSSION QUESTIONS

- What are the most important clinical signs and symptoms to look for during a respiratory assessment in a home setting?
- How can advanced diagnostic tools like spirometry and imaging be effectively utilized in community-based respiratory care?

LESSON TWO: DIAGNOSTIC TOOLS; X-RAYS AND OTHER IMAGING TECHNIQUES

Diagnostic imaging is a crucial aspect of respiratory care, providing valuable information about the structure and function of the respiratory system. This lesson focuses on the use of X-rays and other imaging techniques in diagnosing and managing respiratory conditions.

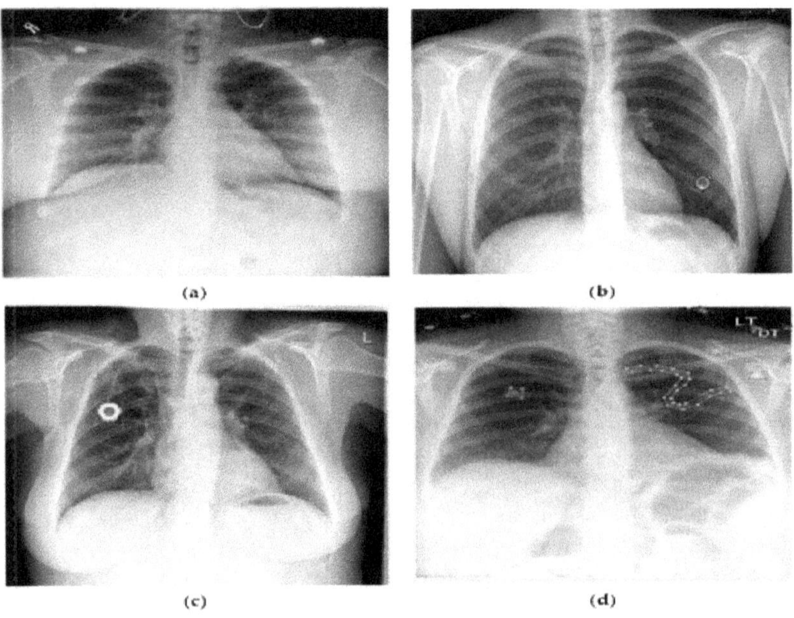

(a)

(b)

(c)

(d)

The Role of Imaging in Respiratory Care

Imaging plays a pivotal role in respiratory care by:

- Identifying Abnormalities: Detecting structural abnormalities, such as tumors, infections, and pleural effusions.
- Guiding Treatment: Providing information that aids in the selection and monitoring of treatment strategies.
- Monitoring Progress: Assessing the effectiveness of treatment and detecting any changes in the condition over time.

Chest X-rays

Chest X-rays are one of the most commonly used imaging techniques in respiratory care. They provide detailed images of the chest, including the lungs, heart, and surrounding structures. Key aspects of chest X-rays include:

- Indications: Chest X-rays are indicated for a variety of respiratory conditions, including pneumonia, chronic obstructive pulmonary disease (COPD), tuberculosis, and lung cancer.
- Technique: The patient stands in front of the X-ray machine, and images are taken from different angles to provide a comprehensive view of the chest.
- Interpretation: Interpreting chest X-rays requires an understanding of normal and abnormal findings. Common abnormalities include infiltrates (suggestive of infection), masses (indicative of tumors), and pleural effusions (accumulation of fluid in the pleural space).

Other Imaging Techniques

In addition to chest X-rays, other imaging techniques are used in respiratory care, including:

- Computed Tomography (CT) Scans: CT scans provide more detailed images than X-rays, allowing for the identification of smaller and more subtle abnormalities. They are particularly useful in diagnosing conditions such as pulmonary embolism, interstitial lung disease, and lung nodules.
- Magnetic Resonance Imaging (MRI): MRI is used less frequently in respiratory care but can provide detailed images of soft tissues, making it useful for evaluating conditions affecting the mediastinum and chest wall.

- Ultrasound: Ultrasound is commonly used to evaluate pleural effusions and guide procedures such as thoracentesis (removal of fluid from the pleural space).
- Positron Emission Tomography (PET) Scans: PET scans are often used in oncology to assess the metabolic activity of lung tumors and detect metastases.

Case Example

Consider a patient with a suspected lung infection. The diagnostic process might involve:

- Initial Assessment: A thorough clinical assessment, including history taking and physical examination, to identify symptoms suggestive of infection.
- Chest X-ray: Performing a chest X-ray to visualize the lungs and identify any infiltrates or other abnormalities.
- CT Scan: If the X-ray findings are inconclusive or if more detail is needed, a CT scan may be performed to provide a clearer picture of the lung structures.

Interpreting Imaging Results

Interpreting imaging results requires expertise and experience. Key principles include:

- Systematic Approach: Using a systematic approach to review the images, ensuring no areas are overlooked.
- Correlation with Clinical Findings: Correlating imaging findings with the patient's clinical presentation and other diagnostic test results.
- Recognizing Normal Variations: Understanding normal anatomical variations and distinguishing them from pathological findings.

Diagnostic imaging is an essential tool in respiratory care. Chest X-rays and other imaging techniques provide valuable information that aids in the diagnosis and management of respiratory conditions.

DISCUSSION QUESTIONS

- How can healthcare providers improve their skills in interpreting chest X-rays to accurately diagnose respiratory conditions?
- What are the limitations of chest X-rays in diagnosing respiratory diseases, and how can these limitations be addressed?

MODULE THREE

LESSON ONE: COMMON RESPIRATORY CONDITIONS AND THEIR MANAGEMENT

Respiratory conditions are diverse and can range from acute infections to chronic diseases. This lesson provides an overview of common respiratory conditions, including their clinical features, diagnostic criteria, and management strategies.

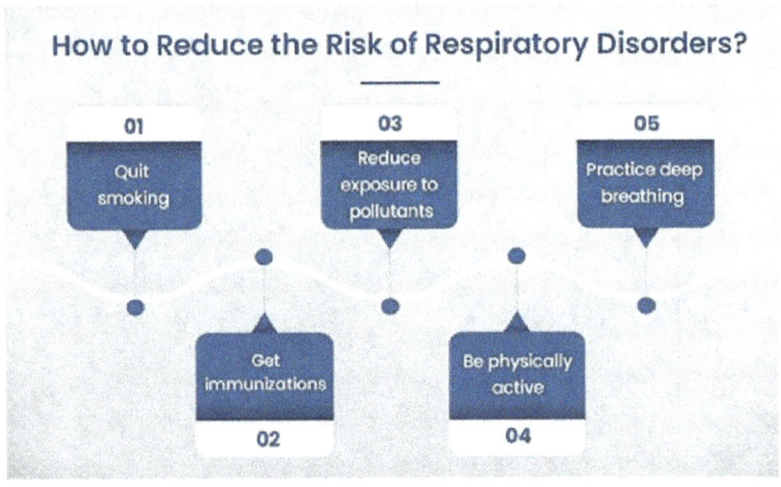

Chronic Obstructive Pulmonary Disease (COPD)

COPD is a chronic inflammatory lung disease that causes obstructed airflow from the lungs. Key aspects of COPD include:

- Clinical Features: Symptoms of COPD include chronic cough, sputum production, and shortness of breath, particularly during physical activities.
- Diagnosis: COPD is diagnosed based on spirometry, which shows a persistent reduction in airflow.
- Management: Management of COPD includes smoking cessation, bronchodilators, corticosteroids, and pulmonary

rehabilitation. Oxygen therapy and surgical interventions may be required for advanced cases.

Asthma

Asthma is a chronic condition characterized by airway inflammation and hyperreactivity. Key aspects of asthma include:

- Clinical Features: Symptoms of asthma include wheezing, shortness of breath, chest tightness, and cough, often triggered by allergens or exercise.
- Diagnosis: Asthma is diagnosed based on history, physical examination, and spirometry, which shows reversible airflow obstruction.
- Management: Management of asthma includes avoiding triggers, using inhaled corticosteroids and bronchodilators, and monitoring lung function.

Pneumonia

Pneumonia is an infection of the lungs that can be caused by bacteria, viruses, or fungi. Key aspects of pneumonia include:

- Clinical Features: Symptoms of pneumonia include fever, cough, chest pain, and difficulty breathing.
- Diagnosis: Pneumonia is diagnosed based on clinical examination, chest X-ray, and laboratory tests such as sputum culture.
- Management: Management of pneumonia includes antibiotics for bacterial infections, supportive care, and sometimes hospitalization for severe cases.

Tuberculosis (TB)

Tuberculosis is a bacterial infection caused by Mycobacterium tuberculosis. Key aspects of TB include:

- Clinical Features: Symptoms of TB include a persistent cough, fever, night sweats, and weight loss.
- Diagnosis: TB is diagnosed based on history, physical examination, chest X-ray, and laboratory tests such as sputum smear microscopy and culture.
- Management: Management of TB includes a combination of antibiotics taken for several months, along with monitoring for drug resistance and side effects.

Lung Cancer

Lung cancer is a malignant tumor of the lungs that is often associated with smoking. Key aspects of lung cancer include:

- Clinical Features: Symptoms of lung cancer include a persistent cough, chest pain, weight loss, and hemoptysis (coughing up blood).
- Diagnosis: Lung cancer is diagnosed based on imaging studies such as chest X-ray and CT scan, followed by biopsy to confirm the diagnosis.
- Management: Management of lung cancer includes surgery, chemotherapy, radiation therapy, and targeted therapies, depending on the stage and type of cancer.

Case Example

Consider a patient with chronic cough and shortness of breath. The diagnostic process might involve:

- Initial Assessment: A thorough history and physical examination to identify symptoms suggestive of COPD.
- Spirometry: Performing spirometry to assess lung function and confirm the diagnosis.
- Management Plan: Developing a comprehensive management plan that includes smoking cessation, medications, and pulmonary rehabilitation.

Understanding common respiratory conditions and their management is essential for healthcare providers. By recognizing the clinical features, diagnostic criteria, and treatment options, providers can deliver effective care and improve patient outcomes.

DISCUSSION QUESTIONS

How do the management strategies for common respiratory conditions like COPD and asthma differ in home versus hospital settings?

What are the most effective approaches for preventing exacerbations of chronic respiratory conditions in community settings?

LESSON TWO: PHARMACOLOGICAL INTERVENTIONS IN RESPIRATORY CARE

Pharmacological interventions are a cornerstone of respiratory care, providing relief from symptoms, reducing inflammation, and improving lung function. This lesson explores the various medications used in respiratory care, including their mechanisms of action, indications, and potential side effects.

Non-Pharmacologic	Pharmacologic
Non-invasive ventilation Invasive mechanical ventilation	Myoresolution
Lung recruitment PEEP selection	Inhaled vasodilators
Tidal volume setting Oxygen and Carbon Dioxide target	Corticosteroids
Prone positioning Extracorporeal assistance	–

Bronchodilators

Bronchodilators are medications that relax the muscles around the airways, making it easier to breathe. They are commonly used in conditions such as asthma and COPD. Types of bronchodilators include:

- Short-Acting Beta-Agonists (SABAs): These medications, such as albuterol, provide quick relief from acute symptoms by relaxing airway muscles.
- Long-Acting Beta-Agonists (LABAs): These medications, such as salmeterol, provide prolonged relief by maintaining airway dilation.
- Anticholinergics: These medications, such as ipratropium, work by blocking the action of acetylcholine, leading to airway relaxation.

- Combination Inhalers: These inhalers combine bronchodilators with corticosteroids to provide both bronchodilation and anti-inflammatory effects.

Corticosteroids

Corticosteroids are anti-inflammatory medications used to reduce airway inflammation and prevent exacerbations. They are commonly used in asthma and COPD. Types of corticosteroids include:

- Inhaled Corticosteroids (ICS): These medications, such as fluticasone, are delivered directly to the lungs to reduce inflammation with minimal systemic effects.
- Oral Corticosteroids: These medications, such as prednisone, are used for short-term management of severe exacerbations.
- Systemic Corticosteroids: These medications are used in more severe cases and can have significant side effects with long-term use.

Leukotriene Modifiers

Leukotriene modifiers are medications that block the action of leukotrienes, which are inflammatory chemicals involved in asthma. They are used as an adjunct therapy in asthma management. Types of leukotriene modifiers include:

- Leukotriene Receptor Antagonists: Medications such as montelukast block leukotriene receptors, reducing inflammation and bronchoconstriction.

Antihistamines

Antihistamines are used to manage allergic symptoms that can exacerbate respiratory conditions such as asthma and allergic rhinitis. Types of antihistamines include:

- First-Generation Antihistamines: These medications, such as diphenhydramine, can cause drowsiness and are typically used for short-term relief.
- Second-Generation Antihistamines: These medications, such as cetirizine, have fewer sedative effects and are used for long-term management.

Antibiotics

Antibiotics are used to treat bacterial infections of the respiratory tract, such as pneumonia and bronchitis. The choice of antibiotic depends on the suspected or confirmed pathogen and the patient's clinical condition. Types of antibiotics include:

- Macrolides: Medications such as azithromycin are often used for respiratory infections due to their broad-spectrum activity and anti-inflammatory properties.
- Beta-Lactams: Medications such as amoxicillin are commonly used for bacterial infections like pneumonia.
- Fluoroquinolones: Medications such as levofloxacin are used for more severe infections or when other antibiotics are ineffective.

Mucolytics and Expectorants

Mucolytics and expectorants are used to manage conditions with excessive mucus production, such as chronic bronchitis. Types of these medications include:

- Mucolytics: Medications such as acetylcysteine help break down mucus, making it easier to expel.
- Expectorants: Medications such as guaifenesin help thin and loosen mucus, facilitating its removal from the respiratory tract.

Case Example

Consider a patient with asthma experiencing frequent exacerbations. The pharmacological management might involve:

- Inhaled Corticosteroids: Prescribing an inhaled corticosteroid to reduce airway inflammation.
- Long-Acting Beta-Agonists: Adding a LABA to provide prolonged bronchodilation.
- Leukotriene Modifiers: Including a leukotriene receptor antagonist to further reduce inflammation and prevent exacerbations.
- Antihistamines: Using an antihistamine to manage any underlying allergies contributing to asthma symptoms.

Pharmacological interventions are critical in the management of respiratory conditions. Understanding the mechanisms of action, indications, and potential side effects of these medications enables healthcare providers to optimize treatment and improve patient outcomes.

DISCUSSION QUESTIONS

- What are the potential side effects of common respiratory medications, and how can they be managed in a home care environment?
- How can healthcare providers ensure medication adherence among patients with chronic respiratory conditions?

MODULE FOUR

LESSON ONE: NON-PHARMACOLOGICAL TREATMENTS AND THERAPIES

Non-pharmacological treatments and therapies play a vital role in the comprehensive management of respiratory conditions. This lesson explores various non-pharmacological interventions, including respiratory therapy techniques, lifestyle modifications, and patient education.

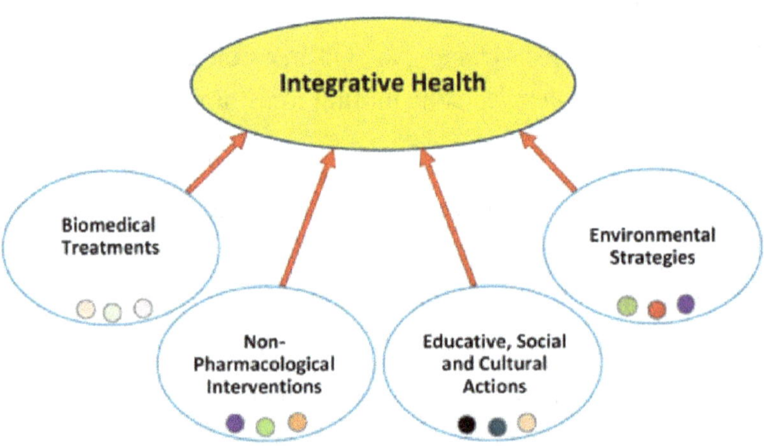

Respiratory Therapy Techniques

Respiratory therapy techniques are essential for improving lung function, clearing secretions, and enhancing overall respiratory health. Key techniques include:

- Chest Physiotherapy: Techniques such as percussion, vibration, and postural drainage help mobilize and clear mucus from the airways.
- Breathing Exercises: Exercises such as diaphragmatic breathing and pursed-lip breathing improve ventilation and reduce breathlessness.

- Incentive Spirometry: Using an incentive spirometer encourages deep breathing and prevents atelectasis (collapse of lung tissue).
- Positive Expiratory Pressure (PEP) Therapy: PEP devices help keep the airways open and facilitate mucus clearance.

Lifestyle Modifications

Lifestyle modifications are crucial for managing chronic respiratory conditions and improving overall health. Key modifications include:

- Smoking Cessation: Quitting smoking is the most important intervention for patients with COPD and other smoking-related respiratory conditions.
- Exercise and Physical Activity: Regular physical activity improves cardiovascular fitness, muscle strength, and respiratory function.
- Healthy Diet: A balanced diet supports overall health and can help manage weight, which is important for respiratory function.
- Avoiding Triggers: Identifying and avoiding environmental and occupational triggers that can exacerbate respiratory conditions.

Patient Education

Patient education is a cornerstone of effective respiratory care, empowering patients to manage their conditions and adhere to treatment plans. Key components of patient education include:

- Understanding the Condition: Educating patients about their respiratory condition, including its causes, symptoms, and potential complications.
- Medication Management: Teaching patients how to use inhalers, nebulizers, and other medications correctly.

- Self-Monitoring: Encouraging patients to monitor their symptoms and recognize early signs of exacerbations.
- Action Plans: Developing personalized action plans that outline steps to take during exacerbations or emergencies.

Pulmonary Rehabilitation

Pulmonary rehabilitation is a comprehensive program that combines exercise training, education, and support to improve the physical and emotional well-being of patients with chronic respiratory conditions. Key components of pulmonary rehabilitation include:

- Exercise Training: Supervised exercise sessions tailored to the patient's fitness level and respiratory condition.
- Education: Informative sessions on respiratory health, nutrition, and coping strategies.
- Psychosocial Support: Counseling and support groups to address the emotional challenges associated with chronic respiratory conditions.

Case Example

Consider a patient with COPD who continues to experience breathlessness despite optimal pharmacological management. The non-pharmacological interventions might include:

- Chest Physiotherapy: Implementing chest physiotherapy techniques to help clear mucus and improve lung function.
- Breathing Exercises: Teaching the patient diaphragmatic breathing and pursed-lip breathing exercises to reduce breathlessness.
- Pulmonary Rehabilitation: Enrolling the patient in a pulmonary rehabilitation program to enhance overall fitness and well-being.

- Patient Education: Providing education on the importance of smoking cessation, medication adherence, and recognizing early signs of exacerbations.

Non-pharmacological treatments and therapies are essential components of comprehensive respiratory care. By incorporating respiratory therapy techniques, lifestyle modifications, and patient education, healthcare providers can significantly improve patient outcomes and quality of life.

DISCUSSION QUESTIONS

- How can respiratory therapy techniques be adapted for use in home settings to manage chronic respiratory conditions?
- What lifestyle modifications can significantly impact the management of respiratory diseases, and how can healthcare providers support patients in making these changes?

MODULE FIVE

LESSON ONE: CASE STUDIES AND PRACTICAL APPLICATIONS

Case studies provide valuable insights into the real-world application of respiratory care principles and techniques. This lesson presents a series of case studies that illustrate the assessment, diagnosis, and management of various respiratory conditions in home and community settings.

CASE STUDY 1: CHRONIC OBSTRUCTIVE PULMONARY DISEASE (COPD)

Patient Profile:

- Age: 65
- Gender: Male
- History: Long-term smoker, diagnosed with COPD 10 years ago

- Presenting Symptoms: Increased shortness of breath, chronic cough with sputum production

Assessment and Diagnosis:

- History Taking: Detailed history of smoking, previous exacerbations, and current medications.
- Physical Examination: Inspection, palpation, percussion, and auscultation revealing diminished breath sounds and wheezing.
- Diagnostic Tools: Spirometry showing reduced FEV1/FVC ratio, chest X-ray indicating hyperinflation.

Management:

- Pharmacological Interventions: Prescribing a combination inhaler (LABA and ICS), short-acting bronchodilator for rescue use.
- Non-Pharmacological Interventions: Smoking cessation program, pulmonary rehabilitation, and patient education on breathing exercises and medication adherence.

Outcome:

- Follow-Up: Improved symptom control, reduced exacerbations, and enhanced quality of life through comprehensive management.

CASE STUDY 2: ASTHMA

Patient Profile:

- Age: 30
- Gender: Female
- History: Diagnosed with asthma in childhood, frequent exacerbations triggered by allergens

- Presenting Symptoms: Wheezing, shortness of breath, chest tightness, particularly during the spring season

Assessment and Diagnosis:

- History Taking: Detailed history of symptom triggers, previous exacerbations, and medication use.
- Physical Examination: Inspection, palpation, percussion, and auscultation revealing wheezing.
- Diagnostic Tools: Spirometry showing reversible airflow obstruction, allergy testing identifying specific allergens.

Management:

- Pharmacological Interventions: Prescribing inhaled corticosteroid and long-acting beta-agonist combination, short-acting bronchodilator for rescue use, and leukotriene receptor antagonist.
- Non-Pharmacological Interventions: Allergen avoidance strategies, use of air purifiers, patient education on inhaler technique and action plan for exacerbations.

Outcome:

- Follow-Up: Reduced frequency of exacerbations, improved asthma control, and better quality of life through tailored management plan.

CASE STUDY 3: PNEUMONIA

Patient Profile:

- Age: 50
- Gender: Female
- History: No significant medical history, non-smoker
- Presenting Symptoms: High fever, productive cough, pleuritic chest pain, and dyspnea

Assessment and Diagnosis:

- History Taking: Detailed history of symptom onset, exposure to sick contacts, and recent travel.
- Physical Examination: Inspection, palpation, percussion, and auscultation revealing crackles and decreased breath sounds in the affected area.
- Diagnostic Tools: Chest X-ray showing lobar consolidation, sputum culture identifying the causative organism.

Management:

- Pharmacological Interventions: Prescribing appropriate antibiotics based on sputum culture results, antipyretics for fever, and analgesics for chest pain.

Non-Pharmacological Interventions: Encouraging rest, hydration, and use of incentive spirometry to prevent atelectasis.

Outcome:

- Follow-Up: Complete resolution of symptoms with appropriate antibiotic therapy, and patient education on preventing future respiratory infections.

These case studies demonstrate the application of comprehensive respiratory care principles in diverse clinical scenarios. By integrating pharmacological and non-pharmacological interventions, healthcare providers can effectively manage respiratory conditions and improve patient outcomes.

DISCUSSION QUESTIONS

- What can healthcare providers learn from case studies to improve the management of respiratory conditions in real-world settings?
- How can personalized care plans be developed and implemented based on the insights gained from case studies?

MODULE SIX

LESSON ONE: PEDIATRIC RESPIRATORY CARE

Respiratory conditions in children present unique challenges and require specialized approaches for effective management. This lesson focuses on the assessment, diagnosis, and treatment of common pediatric respiratory conditions, emphasizing the differences from adult respiratory care.

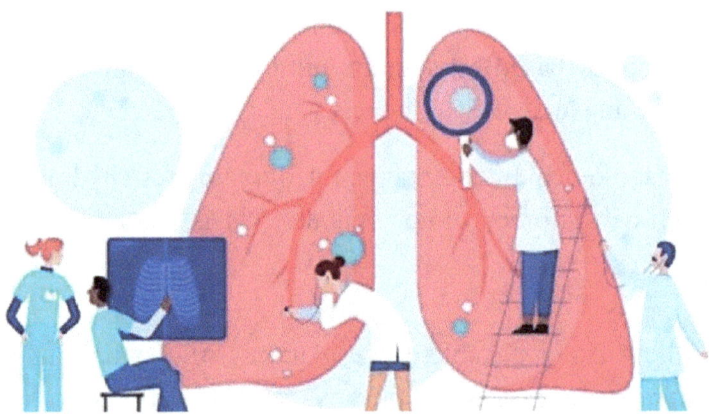

Common Pediatric Respiratory Conditions

Understanding common respiratory conditions in children is crucial for providing appropriate care. These conditions include:

- Asthma: Asthma in children often presents with recurrent wheezing, coughing, and shortness of breath. Triggers can include allergens, exercise, and respiratory infections. Management involves the use of inhaled corticosteroids, bronchodilators, and trigger avoidance.

- Bronchiolitis: Typically caused by respiratory syncytial virus (RSV), bronchiolitis affects infants and young children. Symptoms include cough, wheezing, and difficulty breathing.

Management is usually supportive, including hydration, oxygen therapy, and in severe cases, mechanical ventilation.

- Croup: Characterized by a barking cough and stridor, croup is often caused by viral infections. Treatment includes humidified air, corticosteroids, and in severe cases, nebulized epinephrine.
- Pneumonia: Bacterial and viral pneumonia are common in children, presenting with fever, cough, and difficulty breathing. Diagnosis involves clinical assessment, chest X-ray, and laboratory tests. Management includes appropriate antibiotics for bacterial pneumonia and supportive care for viral infections.
- Cystic Fibrosis: A genetic disorder affecting the respiratory and digestive systems, cystic fibrosis leads to thick, sticky mucus production. Management includes chest physiotherapy, mucolytics, antibiotics, and nutritional support.

Pediatric Assessment Techniques

Assessing respiratory conditions in children requires age-appropriate techniques and a thorough understanding of pediatric physiology. Key components include:

- History Taking: Gathering detailed information about symptom onset, frequency, and triggers, as well as family history and prenatal and birth history.
- Physical Examination: Techniques include inspection, palpation, percussion, and auscultation, with attention to signs such as nasal flaring, retractions, and cyanosis.
- Diagnostic Tools: Use of pulse oximetry, chest X-rays, and spirometry (for older children) to assess respiratory function and identify abnormalities.

Pediatric Treatment Strategies

Treatment of pediatric respiratory conditions involves both pharmacological and non-pharmacological approaches, tailored to the child's age and condition.

- Medications: Use of inhaled corticosteroids, bronchodilators, and antibiotics, with careful dosing and monitoring for side effects.
- Respiratory Therapy: Techniques such as chest physiotherapy, nebulized treatments, and breathing exercises to improve lung function and clear secretions.
- Supportive Care: Ensuring adequate hydration, nutrition, and comfort measures, as well as education and support for families to manage chronic conditions at home.

Case Example

Consider a young child with recurrent episodes of wheezing and cough:

- Initial Assessment: Detailed history taking to identify potential triggers and pattern of symptoms, physical examination revealing wheezing and use of accessory muscles.
- Diagnostic Tools: Spirometry (if age-appropriate) and allergy testing to identify specific allergens.
- Management Plan: Prescribing inhaled corticosteroids and a bronchodilator, developing an asthma action plan, and providing education on trigger avoidance and inhaler technique.

Pediatric respiratory care requires a specialized approach that considers the unique physiological and developmental needs of children. By combining thorough assessment, appropriate treatment strategies, and comprehensive family education, healthcare providers can effectively manage pediatric respiratory conditions and improve outcomes.

DISCUSSION QUESTIONS

- How do the diagnostic criteria and treatment approaches for asthma differ between pediatric patients and adults?
- What are the challenges in managing chronic respiratory conditions like cystic fibrosis in children, and how can healthcare providers address these challenges?

MODULE SEVEN

LESSON ONE: INNOVATIONS AND FUTURE DIRECTIONS IN RESPIRATORY CARE

The field of respiratory care is continually evolving with advancements in technology, research, and clinical practices. This lesson explores recent innovations and future directions that hold promise for improving respiratory care in home and community settings.

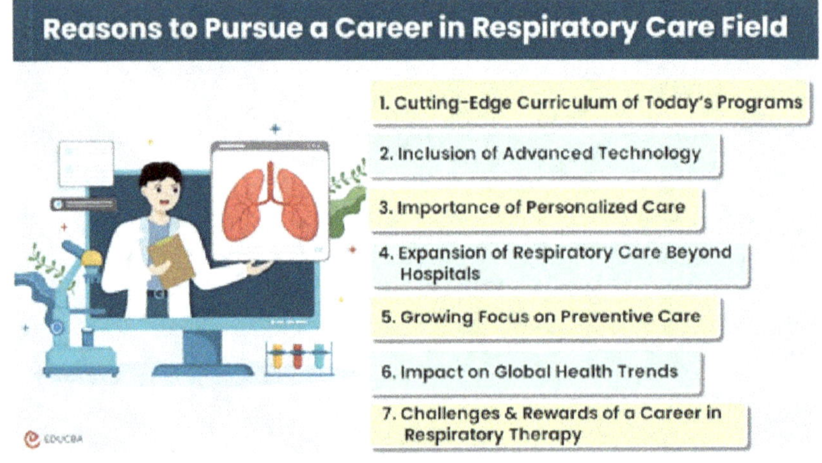

Technological Innovations

Technology is playing an increasingly significant role in respiratory care, enhancing diagnostic accuracy, treatment effectiveness, and patient engagement. Key innovations include:

- Telemedicine: The use of telemedicine platforms allows for remote monitoring, consultation, and management of respiratory conditions, especially in rural or underserved areas. Patients can receive timely care and education without the need for frequent in-person visits.

- Wearable Devices: Wearable technology, such as smart inhalers and respiratory monitors, enables continuous tracking of respiratory function and medication adherence. These devices can provide real-time feedback to patients and healthcare providers, facilitating proactive management.
- Advanced Imaging Techniques: Innovations in imaging, such as high-resolution CT scans and MRI, offer more detailed visualization of the respiratory system, aiding in the early detection and precise diagnosis of conditions.
- Artificial Intelligence (AI): AI algorithms are being developed to analyze imaging data, predict exacerbations, and personalize treatment plans based on patient-specific data. AI can enhance clinical decision-making and improve patient outcomes.

Research and Clinical Advances

Ongoing research is leading to new insights and therapies for respiratory conditions. Key areas of focus include:

- Biologics and Targeted Therapies: The development of biologics and targeted therapies, such as monoclonal antibodies, offers new treatment options for conditions like asthma and COPD, particularly for patients with severe or refractory disease.
- Gene Therapy: Advances in gene therapy hold potential for treating genetic respiratory disorders, such as cystic fibrosis. By correcting the underlying genetic defects, these therapies aim to provide long-term solutions.
- Regenerative Medicine: Research into stem cell therapy and tissue engineering aims to regenerate damaged lung tissue, offering hope for conditions like pulmonary fibrosis and emphysema.

Patient-Centered Care

The shift towards patient-centered care emphasizes the importance of involving patients in their own health management. Key components include:

- Personalized Medicine: Tailoring treatment plans to the individual characteristics of each patient, including their genetic profile, lifestyle, and preferences, to achieve better outcomes.
- Patient Education and Empowerment: Providing comprehensive education and resources to empower patients to take an active role in managing their respiratory conditions. This includes the use of digital health tools, educational apps, and support groups.
- Holistic Approaches: Integrating holistic approaches, such as mindfulness, yoga, and nutritional counseling, into respiratory care to address the overall well-being of patients.

Case Example

Consider a patient with severe asthma managed through a combination of traditional and innovative approaches:

- Initial Assessment: Detailed history taking and physical examination, supported by advanced imaging and genetic testing to identify specific phenotypes and triggers.
- Technological Integration: Use of a smart inhaler to monitor medication adherence and a wearable device to track respiratory function and detect early signs of exacerbations.
- Personalized Treatment: Administration of a biologic therapy tailored to the patient's specific asthma phenotype, alongside traditional inhaled corticosteroids and bronchodilators.
- Patient Engagement: Providing comprehensive education on asthma management, access to a telemedicine platform for

regular follow-ups, and enrollment in a pulmonary rehabilitation program incorporating holistic therapies.

Innovations and future directions in respiratory care offer exciting possibilities for enhancing patient outcomes and quality of life. By embracing technological advancements, research breakthroughs, and patient-centered approaches, healthcare providers can deliver more effective and personalized care for respiratory conditions.

DISCUSSION QUESTIONS

- How can telemedicine and wearable devices be integrated into the management of chronic respiratory conditions to improve patient outcomes?
- What are the ethical considerations and potential challenges associated with implementing gene therapy and regenerative medicine in respiratory care?

CONCLUSION

The management of respiratory conditions in home and community settings is a critical and evolving area of healthcare that demands a comprehensive and multifaceted approach. This book has explored the fundamental aspects of respiratory care, from understanding the anatomy and physiology of the respiratory system to the interpretation of diagnostic tools, and from pharmacological and non-pharmacological treatments to innovative future directions.

The effective management of respiratory conditions begins with a thorough understanding of the respiratory system's anatomy and physiology, allowing healthcare providers to recognize and address various pathophysiological changes. Accurate and timely clinical assessment, supported by advanced diagnostic tools, is essential for identifying respiratory conditions and formulating appropriate treatment plans.

Pharmacological interventions remain the cornerstone of respiratory care, offering relief from symptoms and improving lung function. However, the integration of non-pharmacological treatments, such as respiratory therapy techniques, lifestyle modifications, and patient education, is equally vital in managing chronic respiratory conditions and enhancing patient outcomes.

The landscape of respiratory care is continuously evolving, with new challenges and opportunities emerging. By staying informed about the latest developments, embracing innovative technologies, and focusing on patient-centered care, healthcare providers can significantly improve the management of respiratory conditions in home and community settings, ultimately leading to better health outcomes and quality of life for patients.

REFERENCES

- Barnes, P. J. (2013). *New therapies for chronic obstructive pulmonary disease. Nature Reviews Drug Discovery.*
- Bateman, E. D., et al. (2008). *Global strategy for asthma management and prevention: GINA executive summary. European Respiratory Journal.*
- Bourdin, A., et al. (2010). *Diagnostic value of various techniques for determining asthma in the community. European Respiratory Journal.*
- Bush, A. (2008). P*ediatric asthma: Guidelines and controversies. Annals of Allergy, Asthma & Immunology.*
- Celli, B. R., & Barnes, P. J. (2007). *Exacerbations of chronic obstructive pulmonary disease. European Respiratory Journal.*
- Ferkol, T., & Schraufnagel, D. (2014). *The global burden of respiratory disease. Annals of the American Thoracic Society.*
- Gibson, P. G., et al. (2002). *Asthma management plan improves outcomes for chronic asthma. Thorax.*
- Goldstein, R. S., et al. (1994). *Pulmonary rehabilitation: A review of the evidence. Chest.*
- Levy, M. L., et al. (2009). *Guidelines for the diagnosis and management of asthma: A look at the key differences between pediatric and adult care. British Medical Journal.*
- Li, J. T., et al. (2004). *Diagnosis and management of stable chronic obstructive pulmonary disease: A summary of the evidence. Journal of the American Medical Association.*